I0116312

Hello, Love

The Internet Scammer's Guide to Defrauding Lonely Women on Social Media

Sandra Miller Linhart

LIONHEART GROUP PUBLISHING
PRINTED IN THE USA

Hello, Love

The Internet Scammer's Guide to Defrauding Lonely Women on Social Media

For information regarding permission, email Lionheart Group Publishing: permissions@lionheartgrouppublishing.com

Paperback ISBN: 978-1-938505-24-9

E-Book ISBN: 978-1-938505-23-2

Text copyright © 2017 by Sandra Miller Linhart

Cover art & Design copyright © 2017 by Sandi Linhart.

First Edition ~ October 2017

Published by Lionheart Group Publishing, Colorado, USA

Printed in the USA ~ All rights reserved.

www.lionheartgrouppublishing.com

For the lonely.

Hello, Love

The Internet Scammer's
Guide to Defrauding
Lonely Women on
Social Media

In the Beginning

I assume you have access to the Internet, whether by phone or computer. If you don't have either – or any other way of going on-line – this booklet is not for you. If you do have Internet access, you, my dear, are good to go. Let's get started, shall we?

First, set up a spoof account on social media – any one of them – it doesn't really matter. Honestly, any site will do, even dating sites.

These sites all have relatively easy user-friendly platforms, and if you encounter problems setting one up, each site offers a HELP button – or merely turn to one of your scammer buddy cohorts beside you and request his or her help. Undoubtedly a pro sits not more than twenty feet from you.

Some have suggested a romance-defrauding bot of sorts exists which pulls applicable addresses from social media sites into a big pool of potential victims, from which one can freely fish. As I'm an author of fiction and not a computer guru, I can't answer to that. But it wouldn't surprise me in the least, and makes loads more sense. Much money and havoc can be made through social media if done correctly.

Picture Selection

When it comes to picture selection, the more attractive to the opposite targeted sex the better. Pick an image of a middle-aged (not too young, not too old, a little graying around the temples maybe), physically fit person.

You want your persona to be one not easily passed up by the lonely-hearted. Your goal is to get these vulnerable souls thinking they hit the jackpot. They may finally have a chance with a desirable mate; one who could score a knock-out, but has had his heart broken so many times he's now looking for someone kind, honest, and stable.

Want some good advice? Use a photograph of a high-ranking military official or perhaps even a movie star or one of England's royals. These profile pictures run amok over the Internet and are yours for the copy/pasting. Ignore the fact there are reportedly two million people serving in the US Military today and may recognize the person in the photo. Many of the military members are or have been married at some point in their lives, and have children, parents, siblings, and friends – all of whom know a bit more than just a little about the military (what the ranks are, and how many of the people in higher-ranking positions are, for example).

Also, don't be concerned that Americans (for the most part) are cinephiles and tend to place their favorite actor(s) on a pedestal. Use Brad Pitt's, John Lennon or Marisa Tomei's image as your profile picture. Chances are no one will notice.

Your lonely victim may have not attended the movies in decades and, let's face it – John Lennon isn't likely to release any new music, so you're safe…more than likely.

Name Selection

In some cultures, last names appear first – which is why many Americans ignorantly wonder why so many Koreans are named Kim. The truth is a big segment of the world's population follow this practice.

Along with Korea, places like Hong Kong, Cambodia, China, Hungary, Japan, Madagascar, Vietnam, Taiwan... and parts of India place the family, or last name, before the individual's first name.

With that thought in mind, consider picking a name for your profile picture – go with the surname first to keep consistent with your culture.

If you're using a military member's image as your profile picture ignore the name embroidered on the chest badge – it means nothing. Believe me. Perhaps it was a hand-me-down from another service member?

If you do use the name on the badge, use it as a first name or make up a good first name to go with it. A name like Jesus is always a good one for a Christian or Hispanic-based society like America.

So, to be clear, your name should probably be something like GEN Geesey Jesus... or how we in America like to say General Jesus Geesey. Whatever. Po-tay-toe, pa-tah-toe. As my daughter is wont to say, "You do you, Boo."

Caption Selection

Once you have the perfect profile picture selected, it's time to work on developing an engaging 'about you' section.

In your social media account caption or description, be sure to declare your honesty – because, really, who *cannot* trust someone who blatantly demands "trust me" in describing themselves? Especially Americans. They fall for that shit, man. Dish it out.

Talk about how lonely and trustworthy you are. You may want to add you're looking for an honest soul mate. Say whatever is necessary to get those lonely hearts beating. Be creative and scoop on the sincere sauce...

Or, you may opt to not put anything at all; keep the little lambs guessing. Make them ask for the deets on you; hook 'em with your mysterious ways.

Along with this 'about me' section of your account, remember to load up some random pictures in your content section. Close, advertiser-y shots of roses, puppies, kittens, and wine work well, too.

If your cover story is one of a widow/widower with a kid, put some random kid pics on there. As for whether or not the pictures you post look like the same person, 'close enough' is a good rule of thumb. Lonely people are so desperate they'll ignore most discrepancies.

Some image galleries may have multiple shots of the same person in different situations, so if you're lucky enough to snatch those up, post them – even if your buddy sitting next to you is using the same images.

Don't give it a second thought that all your pictures – whether there be one or twenty – show an identical upload date, or uploaded within days of each other. No American is smart enough to look discerningly at and have the incredulous idea you've been on that social networking site for a mere couple of moments. The vast number of your images make it appear you've been at it for weeks, maybe months even. Americans aren't observant. Really. No worries. Knock yourself out.

Your First Move

...or Pre-Pounce, as we say in the defrauding business.

Wait.

No, really. Simply wait. That's the first step for any predator. And, yes, you are a predator. Admit it, accept it, and embrace it fully. You're after something from these victims – whether it be to launder your dirty money, send you prepaid cards, shower you with undeserved income or to virtually torture and torment – you're not exactly a class-act. You're pretty much scum of the earth, but rest assured, scum of the earth is revered where you come from so no worries there, either.

Yes, Wait. Just wait. Trust me, the moment will come. This is where handy social media networks help you out (or your handy-dandy bot will). Social media sites offer lambs to the slaughter – VICTIM A, NEW TO THIS SOCIAL MEDIA; CLICK TO FOLLOW OR FRIEND? Boom!! You can see her peacefully swimming under your boat, minding her own business. Load your bait onto your tackle and prepare to cast your first line.

Send her a nice, unobtrusive, non-misogynistic introduction like, "Hello, Dear" because, truly, what woman or man doesn't like to be patronized by being called 'Dear'? Or, take a broad step and go all out – call your prey 'Love' – you can practically hear her heart beat all the way in India or Nigeria.

Send her an emoji with hearts for eyes, or winky-kissy face. That'll win her over from the start. Guaranteed!! Because you see, Americans are easy prey and fall for the first heart emoji they see. Every time. Promise. It's the only reason social media outlets created emojis. Honest. Would I lie to you?

Next Logical Step

After the niceties of "Hi, how's your day" get out of the way, jump right in with the questions like "What's your favorite color?" "What do you fear?" or "What do you do, Dear?" because that's not suspect or weird at all. Everyone in America starts off conversations with favorite colors and job descriptions. Yep! You got it. I honestly wouldn't lie to you.

I oftentimes find myself at the bar telling anon-Joe Schmoe sitting beside me that blue just happens to be my favorite color, and I'm afraid of spiders. He doesn't know anything else about me, but those two little tidbits will for sure clue him in to the type of person I truly am.

Or perhaps I gave him a hint to one of my security questions or how to best torment me in the future? Naw, that can't be it. I trust him because he told me to trust him. And he did draw the heart emoji on the bar napkin, so, you know, that there's true love. Soul mate sauce even.

Sob Story

Now, here's the important part. You'll need to come up with a viable reason to need help from this kind and caring person without appearing to be weak or needy.

First, you'll want to pick out an impressive, well-paying career (If you've already settled on a military career, skip this section). Let's see... what could that be. Oh, I know! A doctor... or an engineer. Doesn't matter what type of doctor or engineer, simply say 'doctor' or 'engineer' and the little lamb will swoon.

Your prey won't consider for even the slightest moment that doctors, engineers, and even military officers had to pursue higher educations, and therefore more than likely speak and write the English language fluently. You're a freakin' doctor!! She'll be blinded by this impressive light.

Be sure to let her know you're currently working in Syria, West Africa, Middle East, or on some peacekeeping mission with the United States military – don't forget to mention that to her in your introduction. The sooner she knows that about you, the better.

Ensure to ask her age, and then make your age close to hers – give yourself a ten-year circumference around her age. Never mind if your picture looks like you're 36 – say you're 56 if she's 55. Thank her for the compliment when she comments on how young you look, and answer in kind.

Then, and here's the biggie – let her know your spouse died in some kind of accident, or she left you for your best friend who is an engineer. The most popular accidents to use are 'car' or 'fire' accidents, apparently. Plane crashes show up now and again so feel free to use that as an excuse to off the co-parent of your semi-orphaned children.

Use the term 'late' to show how learned you are. Tell your intended victim something like 'my wife was late in a fire accident' or 'my husband was late in a plane crash.' Talk about how much you miss your spouse and you haven't even tried looking for a soul mate replacement until now. Then tell your lamb how pretty his or her smile is, or how you want to be BFFs immediately and get to know everything about them.

Let your new soul mate know you have one (or two – up to you) kid(s) in the six-to-sixteen age range. If you say your child is a military member you can put him in his twenties. You can easily construct a dilemma for his peril in which she may need to send him money.

The younger-aged offspring will come in handy later on when you relay they're in danger and need immediate monetary help, or perhaps you'd come to see your lamb if only you had enough money for [fill in the blank]. Could she be a dear and help you out?

But we cover that in one of the next section, don't we? First, we have to pluck our lamb away from the herd and out of the watchful eye of your government.

Culling from the Herd

At the end of the first day of communication, or perhaps the beginning of the second day – depending on how receptive your victim is to your advances, request they download the Viber phone application, or go onto hangouts or VPN for more privacy.

This maneuver is two-fold in nature. Not only does it pull them off the social media from which you can be reported or blocked by a previous victim… uh, soul mate, and thereby lose communication with the fish circling your line, this puts your little lamb onto a cross-platform VoIP (voice over Internet protocol) or other applications which are not restricted or monitored by any government.

Having your soul mate culled, or separated from the herd gives you another huge advantage. You can contact them at any time or place as the free talk and text application, Viber has no call-blocking option. They can't ignore you. You can also log your calls and received messages to consult at will, so you'll be able to refresh your memory on what you've already told them. This is important, as you the more adept you are at this, the more fish you'll have on your line at any given time, and the easier it will be turning your fish into lambs. Viber also allows you to share your images and texts with more than one contact at a time, too, so bonus!

If she or he resists downloading an app, ask for their phone number. This request is strategically placed only after the Viber refusal. By having her cell phone number, you have the most access to her personal life. You can text, talk, and torture – plus you now have a medium of which your soul mate will not likely rid – any time soon.

The second advantage of having your target's phone number is you can ensure this person isn't cat-fishing you in some way. You'll be 100% sure she's not a shill, detective, or fellow scammer.

Going in for the Kill

Some of your pals get impatient and get to this step on the first or second day. I would advise against that course of action.

Wait at least three days before you ask your new love to get you a prepaid card because you're stuck at work and can't, what? sign in on your computer from work, or from the phone you're contacting her with? Oh, that's right. Americans are stupid.

If you chose military as your occupation, you can ask her for money for your leave papers so you can visit her, or some such nonsense.

Most Americans won't know the workings of their own military, so they'll be unaware a military member doesn't have to pay for leave, or have someone else sign them out. Tell her you have no soap, food, or other necessity, but can buy some if only you had the money to do so – everything is so expensive in West Africa and the President messed up your pay… again.

...The Harsh Scam

If your luck in engaging a more lucrative relationship with your soul mate is waning, or never took hold in the first place, you may want to take a completely different approach. Some scammers in your position prefer to go for the terror tactic aspect of this manipulation.

If, after all your hard work to defraud her she doesn't respond or stops responding to your pleas or demands, terrorize her. This is your most logical step forward. After all, this asshole wasted your valuable time. Forget that you approached her with lies from the beginning, that your profile and story are intricate fabrications – she dissed you, man! Go for the jugular! Ruin this person's life and make her ultimately pay in other ways.

For instance, you asked her what she fears most. By delving a bit deeper into those fears early on, you'll be able to use these confidences against her when she displeases you and has become no longer monetarily useful to you. Email or text her videos of what scares her, stuff like that. Keep it up for weeks and months, even. Break her. She deserves it for not falling for your scam.

Tongue out of Cheek

Loneliness is one of the biggest game-changing emotions out there, in my humble opinion. It's amazing what we'll do for a little kindness and attention from another warm body.

There is no age limit on loneliness. I've been lonely as a child, a teenager, a young adult, and now into my fifties. The bastards who prey on this forgotten slice of population know exactly what they're doing. Loneliness is not something to be ashamed of, and neither is falling for one of these serial Don Juans.

The Internet scammer tells us things he or she thinks we want or need to hear. They prey on our insecurities and loneliness. Unfortunately, they're exceptional at it because they've practiced. With each victim, they get more savvy – win or lose the heart they seek. Sometimes it's hard to tell until after they've earned our trust. By that time, it's hard to admit we've made a mistake. We may have already sent them money, given them too much personal information or just plain invested too much time and heart muscle on the creep.

The good news is there are myriad tells to alert us to their fraudulent profile. The bad news is we need to look at our Don Juan's story objectively and admit to ourselves we've been scammed. That's a hard pill to swallow, but in order to stop this new vein of crime, it needs to be reported – the word spread so other women (and men – this is not a gender specific crime) are aware they could be exploited.

The number one tell of a fraudulent profile is the age of the profile. Most of these scammers get blocked on a regular basis so they have to start fresh often. If they're blocked, they lose all of the victims they've been grooming, which is why they work so hard right away to get us, their lambs, onto another message platform almost immediately.

Number two, the images they have posted are loaded in one day, or over the span of only a few days. Most have no personal correlations to anything other than stock photo shots of flowers, animals, or overt images of Christian-based religions (praying hands, an adorned cross, etc.). Think about your friends' images – are these the types of items they post?

There may be congruent shots of kid and dad showing smiling, happy faces. Don't let that fool you. It's extremely easy to go to someone's profile page and copy/paste their images, videos, and photos. The more experienced (and harder to expose) scammers are quite adept at this.

If the messages are in broken English, please keep in mind all career-oriented individuals (officer in the military, doctors, and engineers) have had secondary education of some sort (Bachelor's or Master's degree), if not a PhD, and are more than likely proficient writers and speakers. A true professional's sentence structure will remain constant, and flow like you'd expect someone who's lived here all his or her life – which is what these scammers declare.

Punctuation is tricky. Oftentimes we Americans leave out punctuation in texts and messages, because it's quick and easy. But if our new starry-eyed soul mate is capitalizing odd words for no apparent reason, or putting commas instead of periods, we have to think to ourselves why he'd go through the extra trouble to do it incorrectly. It takes as much key-stroke-power and time to do it right.

As of today's date, there are no military peacekeeping missions currently in Syria or West Africa. Additionally, all peacekeeping operations are typically led by the UN, and if a soldier is boots on ground it's more than likely not for keeping the peace.

At no time should a military member (especially an officer) require money for a leave voucher, or living expenses, or anything. POTUS, regardless of who is in office, never has had anything to do with military monthly income (payday) and therefore cannot deny a soldier his pay. Neither can Congress, which is the entity that determines military pay schedules. If the soldier is active duty in good standing, he has a contract with the United States Department of Defense and is guaranteed pay (and other considerations like healthcare, housing, food, etc.).

If you don't know insignia on the military uniform, it's not hard to check. If someone with four stars on his shoulder boards is telling you he's a Colonel in the military, a quick google will show the image is that of a much higher-ranking officer. Of which the US military has only twenty-four active four-star officers by statute. That's what I'd call slim pickins. IF one of these gentlemen were to contact you, one look at their on-line bio will destroy your scammer's cover story. Be vigilant. Keep in mind high-ranking military officers aren't typically on social media platforms.

If your new guy tells you he's with the United States military, ask what branch. Military members have a frienemy rivalry between branches, and have for years. They're proud of their 'team' and don't like to be confused as being on a rival one. 'I work for the United States military' is not something a true military member would say. If your scammer offers a branch, take the time to check the branch he mentioned has the rank and title he professes to be.

Search engines are our friends and can keep us out of sticky situations if we take the time to investigate what we're being told. Loneliness can make us act out of expectation and anticipation of a lasting relationship and will blind us to the glaring discrepancies in our new friend's story.

Ask what rank they hold. If he says he's a Lieutenant or above, ask where he got his commission (became an officer). An NCO (Non-commissioned officer) is not technically an officer, it's a high-ranking soldier; corporal and sergeant – the leaders of the troops. Download a graph depicting military branches and ranks. These are available on-line and will come in handy if you continue to seek love from a social media site.

If you truly want to stump the creep posing as a military member, ask for his MOS (military occupational specialty, or job title for all services except the Air Force, which is AFSC). If he answers right away, check out what the proffered MOS code means, and ask him for detailed information about his job.

For instance, if your dreamboat says he's 71L, google it and discern whether or not a 71L has any business on the sand in Syria. If your dude says 'Infantry' – that's suspect. Soldiers typically don't state their division as an occupation when asked.

If they take a while to answer, your Don Juan is more than likely looking it up. All soldiers know their MOS, and when asked a pointed question will answer immediately in kind – believing you know what you're asking or you wouldn't have asked it that way.

One last thing. There is no such thing as a 'secret divorce' – all civil court records are public unless a judge orders them sealed in whole or part. The chances of a divorce being deemed personal enough to be 'secret' are about as good as me having a date tonight: Ain't gonna happen. If a high-ranking official in the United States military contacts you and says he's divorced, but you do a quick google that shows him to be married, you're being scammed – and that's no secret.

Proof is in the Pudding

The following transcripts are from actual conversations from contacts over the span of one day (25 September 2017). I left the spelling, grammar and context as is to give the real feel of the broken way these scammers write.

The images and names of the social media accounts are undoubtedly stolen. The people portrayed in them are not the individuals who contacted me.

The use of these profile names is for educational purposes only and are not intended to harass or further distress the silent victims in these cons – the persons whose images and names are being used to perpetrate scams. Therefore, I'll not publish any images but do have them digitally stored for verification if needed, and have offered a brief description of each image sent.

* * *

Collins.ford.1

Greetings Madam, hope you're Strong and Having a Good time

[Notice the use of random capitals.]

-Good morning

Good morning my Love, How are you?

[Boom! Second message to me and I'm already his love.]

-I'm well, and you?

I'm Fine. So happy you Replied me.

Please truly who are you?

[Who speaks like this?]

-I'm me. I don't know what else to say

Okay Darling.

[I'm not sure – did I go up or down in his esteem. Does 'darling' rank higher than 'love'?]

I'm General Collins Ford. A military Doctor.

[No doc in the military says 'military doctor' – they say branch-specific doctor.]

Originally form San Bernardino California. Currently in Kabul, Afghanistan. For Peace Keeping Medical.

Sandra Miller Linhart

[Peace Keeping Medical – WTF is that?]

-Which branch?

[Long pause – about fifteen minutes.]

I'm Medical Surgeon, and Eye ophomologica. I'm working as a medical aid. I don't go to battle any more.

[Oh, that branch. I've never heard of it. I've also never heard of a doctor working as a medical aid, but I'm not the brightest tool in the shed.]

Kisses

[I should have explained to him I rarely kiss on the first date.]

-Cool. That must be lonely being away from your family. Are you married or have kids?

Yeah, I miss my Wife.

But I'm widowed now. I have two Kids.

[Boom! Sob story beginning.]

-Oh I'm so sorry. How did your wife die?

-What are your kids' ages?

I Lost my Late wife to a Fire Accident

[Lost my Late wife? Hrm...what exactly was she late for? Fire accident, seriously? This won't be the first time I hear this term today.]

My Daughter is 6 years old, My Son is 19 years old.

-How long ago did your wife die?

[Long pause – about twenty minutes.]

My wife died 19 years ago. Same year she gave birth to my Only Son.

[And God so loved the world...]

The Daughter I Call mine, She's Adopted.

[I don't know of many single high-ranking officers who successfully adopt a child, especially in their sixties.]

-Wow. You raised your daughter AND son all by yourself. I am impressed.

-I'm sure it was especially difficult while being in the military

[Long pause – over an hour.]

It's Difficult without a wife, to take care of children. That of my Son was worse.

[The cadence and structure of his sentences are off, and not those of an educated American, more of an English as a second language.]

I nurtured him from infant.

I gave him feeding bottle. So you can see what I have been going through. For years.

I don't have any option than to play the role of Caring Father that I'm. Till the Day, God blesses me with a Good woman.

[Random and incorrect punctuation – I'm chatting with a General, here. A GEN has to have a Bachelor's under

his belt, if not a Master's – and, from my understanding, no officer has easily achieved the rank of GEN without having graduated from a military academy.]

-As a single mom, I know exactly what you've been going through. It's not easy.

Oh Darling. I know how you feel. How do you cope without a Husband, How Old are your Children?

-Well, now they're adults but for a very long time it was just me paying the bills and keeping them fed and safe

Even me that's Wealthy, I have all I need. Sometimes I do borrow just to get my Children nice things. Because I'm not always around. I'm far away. I Provide for them. I have a Good Job.

[Dropped clue so when he asks you for money, it's only for his children and to buy them nice things because he's not around.]

How about you Dear, what's the nature of your Job?

[Nature of my job? Hrm. Not sure I've heard it put that way since my great-grandma died.]

-I'm a paralegal

[Long pause]

Hmm, That's Awesome

[Awesome? It feels like I'm chatting with a young person who slips out of character every now and again.]

A paralegal is an individual, qualified by education, training or work experience, who is employed or retained by a lawyer, law office, corporation, governmental agency, or other entity.

[Straight off of dictionary.com?]

Hope I'm Right

-You're right

So how much do you enjoy your Job?

Is it your Dream job, or something Else?

-I'm good at it, that makes it rewarding.

Awesome

how old are your kids?

-They're all grown and have their own lives

-I have to get some work done. It was nice chatting with you.

Okay Darling, Kisses

[Wow. That escalated quickly.]

[Over the course of the evening he wrote some messages about how he wanted to still chat and where'd I go – don't leave him stranded. When I woke up this morning the last message he wrote above had disappeared and was replaced with a "Hi." 26 Sept 2017]

Hi

Sandra Miller Linhart

-Good morning

Where have you been? I'm happy to here from you

**-I had a deadline at work then went to bed.
Thanks for thinking of me.**

You're Welcome. Why won't I think about you.
You're Decent to me.
[I'm actually not.]
You Deserve Love, Care, and Affection.

**-Thank you. But how do you know that? You
don't really know me**

I want to know you more. Please. Even though
we are not in a Relationship, I just want us to be
the best of friends.

**-So tell me a little about yourself. What was
your childhood like? Any siblings?**

[Long pause.]
Oh thanks for asking. You're truly caring.
I will tell you.
[Picture of two olive-skinned kids; typical family-type portrait.]
That's me Being Carried by my Late Elder sister
*[What do you call your 'elder' sibling? And when's the
last time you referred to anyone you lost as 'late'?]*
Our parents died when we were still very young

and tender. Grandparents Raised me up.

[Tender? Seriously? Eating young ones, are we? Also, notice his grandparents didn't just raise him – they raised him up.]

My Grand Father was a Soldier. He persuaded me into becoming a Military man. Back then I used to be a Rock Star before I joined the Military.

[Rock Star denotes fame – not simply 'I was in a garage band back then' and most grandfathers persuade young ones to 'join the military' not become a military man.]

[Picture of, I think, John Lennon holding (more than likely) Julian.]

This is me, with my Son, After the Death of my Wife

I raised him, My Son.

[Yeah, you said that already.]

[Picture of three girls playing on swings in yard. -No explanation given.]

[Picture of a young girl standing with older woman.]

This is me and my Grand mother

[Picture of young girl holding a rifle.]

This is me here too

[Picture of rock star playing a guitar on stage from I'm guessing the 70s – maybe Peter Frampton? The image is fuzzy, making it hard to see who it is.]

This is me too. Back then, when I was a Rock Star.

[Think about anyone you ever knew who played in a local, or semi-popular band. What do they call themselves? Rock Stars?]

-Wow. You had an interesting life. What was the name of your band? Maybe I listened to you when I was younger? That'd be so cool.

Yeah back then, I was not Recognized, I was a Local.

[So...not a 'star' exactly?]

Only popular in the military.

I organized shows back then for military men.

[So... you were the USO?]

Before finally I joined the military. I'm Grateful to God, For my Life. God is Faithful.

[...or Allah 'amin – this is not something American Christians typically say. They tend to say, 'God is good' or 'God bless you.' A military officer doesn't exactly 'join' the military.]

I have a Good Life, I'm Rich, Powerful, and Influential.

[Earlier he said he had to borrow to get things for his children.]

-Sounds like you've had and done it all.

-When did you get your medical degree?

When I was 34 years of Age

[The last time I heard anyone say they were 'x years of Age,' I wasn't even born.]

-How old are you now?

I'm 63 years old.

I was born 1954 September 7

*[The US military does **not** write dates in this manner.]*

> **-You just recently had a birthday. Happy Birthday.**

Yes. Thanks Dear.

> **-Too bad you couldn't spend it with your son. That makes me sad**

Not just with my Son, With a Wife too. I miss my Wife.

[Yeah, you said that.]

How old are you?

> **-55**

> **-I'm really enjoying our chat but I have to get work done or I'll be fired. We can chat later?**

Hmm, That's nice.

Yes we can. I enjoy chatting with you too.

> **-Bye**

I feel Good chatting with you?

[I'm sure you do.]

Yes, I'm Sure

[This is a random comment, response to which

I'm unsure.]

Please do not fail to notify me. Okay

[Think of the structure of this sentence. Would an American GEN/Doctor talk like this?]

-Ok

[No further contact.]

* * *

Gen Dunford @ Dunford4USA

Hello Beautiful,

I go through your profile and saw some potential that i love, You are such a beautiful woman and cute too, I would like us to chat and get to know each other more, Kindly write to my email address below so that i get back to you on there with everything about me, I am also on hangout too, I look forward to hearing from you soon through my email address below, God bless you.

My email:

Gendunford59@gmail.com

General Dunford also contacted me on another social media platform with pretty much the same message. When I said I thought he was married (he is), he told me he's going through a secret divorce. Unfortunately, this conversation was early on and I didn't realize how widespread the problem of Internet scammers was becoming, so I didn't save his message. But, I did forward it on to the official Joint Chiefs of Staff social media page. I don't know if they did anything about it, though.

General Dunford is the Chairman of the Joint Chiefs of Staff, and more than likely has little time to schmooze me, or anyone else for that matter, on social media.

* * *

mike_ayer122

Hello

                    -Is it Mark Amber or Mark Ayer?

Mike Ayers
Why ask?

                    -It shows up as both. Just wondering

[His profile page has him listed as 'Ayer' and 'Amber.']
Ok
Where are you from?

                    -Colorado. You?

Am from California

                    -Whereabouts?

But not in the USA now
Duty call
[That's not what soldiers call deployment, unless he

meant to say 'duty calls.']
Where do you work Ma?

-Where were you born?

-Ma? I'm a paralegal

-And where are you currently?

Born in California am in Iraq now

-What city born?

[Long pause.]
San Francisco

-Nice. Beautiful there

Yea
So how's life

-Pretty good. No complaints. How long have you been in Iraq?

Well for a few months now
[Well – along with OK this is a pretty good indication you're speaking to a scammer. You'll find out later this guy says he's a Captain.]
2months
And how's work?

**-Meh. Work's work. It beats the desert tho.
Is it starting to cool down for you guys?**

[Weather.]

Well gun fight often so its hot here

[Action, and notice the 'well' again.]

Hope to come home alive to my son

**-Me, too. Are you married? How old is
your son?**

-Is he in Cali?

In Cali

He is 10

Lost my wife 4 years ago

*[People need to get a better handle on their wives, I'm
thinking. They lose them left and right.]*

You have a family

**-I have grown kids. How'd you lose
your wife?**

-Is your son with your parents, or?

Wife died in a car crash

Well my child with my mum

[English term – not much used in Cali.]

Well she is so old I got a nanny in the house

[Well]

Sandra Miller Linhart

-How old are you?

Well am 45

-What rank are you?

Am a captain

[His profile picture shows the ranking of a staff sergeant. Enlisted ranks cannot rise to officer without entering special programs in today's military. If you're enlisted, you're more than likely going to stay that way throughout your career unless you take some mighty big steps to advance to officer status.]

-What's your MOS?

[No further communication from him.]

* * *

Geeseymorgan11:

Hello

-Hello

How are you doing?

-Good. And you?

I'm fine thank you
nice to meet you
Where are you from?

-Wyoming

-You?

I am GEN.Geesey jesus of the united state military presently reassigned to Syria for a 3 months assignment which happen to be my last assignment before I retire from the united state military and I have spent 30 days here now and I have just a couple of mouth to live here in the camp before I retire am 59 years old

[Wow. Teleprompter speech, much? Notice the transposed name and the misspelling of United States multiple times – also, no branch mentioned. If you know anyone in the military you know they're true to their branch. Not one will just say 'military.' They'll give you the entire 'Hoorah' branch. Also his profile name says Morgan, not Jesus. Ask yourself, if this man is educated why the random punctuation?]

are you married with kids?

-I have kids but am not married. You?

Well I divorced three years and a son who is also a soldier like me he is presently with the joint military force in Iraq, he is 25 years old

How old are you?

-55

That's nice

-Where did you get your commission?

[Long pause – over an hour.]

honestly I'm new here online looking for a soulmate, a nice and caring wman to spend the rest of my life with happily

[Totally leaves me out of your search perimeter, buddy.]

I'm a General officer from the United State Oakton Virginia

[Oh, yeah. I've heard of many officers receiving commission from there. Not! Additionally, Generals in any branch of the military do not typically refer to themselves as a general officer in conversation.]

what is your occupation?

[Quick question. When you want to know where someone works, how do you phrase that conversationally? Think about it.]

-Paralegal. Cool. Virginia. That's a nice place.

-Did you get your degree from USMC Uni there?

[There is no USMC Uni in VA or anywhere else. This was a trick question.]

[Long pause – about forty-five minutes.]

Why, everything is comfram and very well ok

[No freaking idea what confram means, but notice the phrase 'very well ok' – it's often repeated by scammers.]

What is your occupation?

[Second time asked.]

-Paralegal

That's a nice job

Can we be friends and know better about each other

-Yes

Sandra Miller Linhart

Are you serious

[This question confused me. It makes no sense what-so-ever.]

-I don't know what that means

Have you meet any military online before?

[Have I meet any military? Not the way ANY American would phrase that question – especially a military member.]

-Serious about being friends? Yes, why?

-No, I don't think so

Will you like to marry a military officer?

[Ha! Been there, done that.]

-If I loved him

You sound so nice and interesting and i will love to know you better

Are you on Hangout?

[Culling from the herd.]

-No. I'm techno challenged. My kids laugh at me. I've only started using [social media] and that's really all my phone can handle. Plus I'm at work.

Can you download now so we can have more frivacy on there

-No. I'm at work

So when will you be free to do that

-I would have to get my kid's help and she's gone for two weeks

-We can just chat on here. It's pretty private

-I'd like to get to know you better

Can I have your number so we can text message, I'm not that use to [social media]

-It's the office phone and I'm not allowed to use it for personal. I don't own my own mobile. I'm not too good at [social media] either. We can learn together to be better at it.

Well if that is what you want

-Okay

[No further comments from him.]

* * *

Randleonardo

Hello how are you doing and how is the weather treating you out there?

-Coldish. You?

I'm doing great, Nice hearing from you I'm Leonardo from Las Vegas and you?

-I live in Colorado. What do you do in Vegas?

Well I work with the Exxon Mobil and have work with them for years now

[Sentence structure; not American-born.]

I'm currently in West Africa for a drilling contract I'm an engineer working with shell company here in the Pacific Ocean

[Um... sweetie, the west coast of Africa doesn't touch the Pacific Ocean. Color me confused. Also, every time I hear the term 'engineer' I think of a train conductor – is that just me, or?]

Colorado is a very nice place to visit you know

[It's also a nice place to live.]

For how long have you been living over there if I may ask?

-**Quite a while. Moved then moved back. How long are you in W Africa?**

-**Are you married?**

I have been here for 8 months and I lost my wife years ago in a fire accident

[Yet another fire accident – what are the chances?]

-**Oh how horrible. House or car? Do you have kids?**

Car accident, I have two kids Sharon and Lewis and Sheron is the eldest she is 16 years old and Lewis is 14 years old

[So, which is it? Sharon or Sheron?]

Are you married and how many children do you have?

-**Divorced. I have two kids but they are adults. How old are you?**

I'm 65 years years old and you?

-**55. Wow. You had kids really late in life**

-**You don't look 65. You look really young. Nice.**

[Honestly, by his profile picture he looks to be in his mid-forties.]

Thanks for compliment

Do you work and how long have you been working?

[Uh, noneya?]

-I've been working since 14 years old. I'm a paralegal.

[I realized at this point I was changing my speech pattern so he – a non-American – could better understand me. I almost showed my hand.]

-I wasn't a paralegal at 14 but I got my degree as an adult

[I thought it was funny...]

Ok nice to know must say you are a very hard working woman and you kids will be proud of you

Tell me what is your favorite color?

[I don't know why many seem to ask this bizarre question. We're not in grade school any longer. Perhaps they have access to my personal accounts that require security questions?]

Mine is green

-Azure.

-Why do you ask that?

[No further communication from him.]

* * *

Raymondrodney22:

Now this guy is extremely smooth – had I not already been scammed so many times, I may have been conned by him – probably not, but I can see where a woman could fall for his charm. Plus, the image he chose is one of an exceptionally nice-looking man:

Hello Sandra [inserted heart-eyed emoji]

-Hello

How are you?

-I'm well. And you?

Am fine

So where are you fine?

[He said he was fine...I said I was well.]

-Colorado. You?

Am from Washington dc

[Not many people I know leave off the pronoun but keep the verb when truncating communication.]

Nice to meet you

-Nice to meet you

So could you tell me a bit of you?

[He uses 'so' a bit too much, but we do that when we're getting to know someone. Still, it seemed a bit off in this sentence.]

-Not much to tell. Divorced mother of two

OK that's good..well am single father and have being divorced for about 3 years now and I have a lovely daughter Stephanie she's 9 years old.

[First tell – OK, second tell – single father with young kid.]

-What's your name?

Am Raymond

[He keeps leaving off the personal pronoun but keeps the verb, which is disconcerting but acceptable, I suppose.]

You Sandra ?

[Um, yeah. You already called me that at the beginning. Me Tarzan?]

-Yes

-How old are you?

Can you guess my age?

How old are you?

-I guess 44. Am I right?

Lol no

How old are you?

-You first. How old?

I am 57 years old

[Seriously, his pic looks like he's mid-forties.]

You?

-55

-Are you friends with your ex?

So uhm have you not met any man you fancy before on this sight

[Fancy – European term.]

-Well, no. Because this really isn't a dating site so I don't expect to find one really

Alright,good to hear, cause I like you and I really want to be serious with you

[So soon?]

And no...my ex, I don't even see her no more

Heard she moved to another city with her new husband, last year.

-Are you currently in Wash DC?

[Long pause.]

I am in berlin@the moment

-Why?

-What do you do for a living?

[Long pause.]

I work for a shipping company and was recently made director of operations here in berlin

-Where is Stephanie while you're in Berlin?

She's with me

Can't have her too far from me

-That's actually cool. Does she speak German?

I love her so much and I can't bear the thought of her being too far from me

[...and one more time, with feeling.]

Na she's still getting to the new environment

We just moved here 2 months ago

-How long are you going to be there?

I don't know yet, But if I have a good reason to I can when I want

You know all these year, its just been me and my daughter Stephanie... All we have is each other but I have been searching for the right woman to settle down with

[In for the kill. It amazes me how fast they work. What's

his daughter's name again, because he seriously hasn't mentioned it enough.]

-A man as nice looking as you I'm surprised you haven't found anyone

I must admit I have met a couple of women along the way but none of them are really serious with me,so I just lost hope on finding anyone that would really love me.

-I actually have no response to that

You don't have to say anything yet
I just hope,you find a space in your heart for me.

-Honestly I don't know you well enough yet

Alright
You will get to know me well enough dear
[Dear! There it is!]
What do you do for a living??

-I'm a paralegal

That's very nice
What do you do for fun??
What's your favourite restaurant and meal??
[European spelling.]

-Fun? I like hiking and camping.

-Favorite restaurant? Don't really have just one. I like all foods.

-Were you born and raised in the US? [I asked him this because of his spelling of favorite]

[Long pause.]

-Do you have a favorite food?

I was born and raised in Charlotte nc

Yeah I love Chinese foods

[Plural?]

And pizza

What's your favorite colour??

[Again, the European spelling.]

Also do you love flowers??

-Azure

-And, yes. Who doesn't love flowers? (blushing smiley face)

-What's yours?

Lol

My favourite colour is purple

And I love purple rose, which is really rear

-Yes, very pretty

Yeah, its so beautiful

-What time is it in Berlin?

[Long pause.]

-I was in Germany once about this time of
year. Are the leaves changing yet?

How cold is it?

12:25 am, I am supposed to be in bed

-Do you have to work in the morning

I still here cause of you

- (smiley emoji) please forgive

-I'll let you go. Nice chatting with you.

No, it's not a problem
I told you before, I like you alot
I am ready to stay up if it would make you happy
I resume work at the dorks by 10:00

-I should try to get some work done. We can
chat more tomorrow.

Alright dear nice meeting you
Take good care of your self

-**Ditto**

Hugs and kisses. Bye.

[Escalated to hugs and kisses...]

[26 Sept 2017]

Good morning to you dear... I just woke up and you first thing that came into my mind... sending you hugs and kisses to brighten your day... hope you have a wonderful day [blue ribbon wrapped heart]

-**Good morning**

-**How was your work day**

It's going well dear

Hope you good?

And how is work going?

-**I'm good**

-**Thank you**

-**Just started work. So far going well**

OK dear that's good

So have you had breakfast yet?

-**I don't typically eat breakfast. Just coffee**

Aww that's cool

I really do love coffee in the morning

So dear how many hours do you work today?

-I work until the current project is done. Sometimes, like yesterday because I was on here more than I should be, that means 10 or so

[...researching and making notes of these conversations.]

Ok that's ok

[This is reoccurring text the scammer does, probably without thinking. I picture him or her writing down responses or thinking of something else to ask, so they put in a filler to keep you engaged.]

So dear please don't stress yourself too much ok

-Thank you. I won't – but I do need to get some work done this morning. Perhaps we can chat this afternoon?

Yeah dear

I was wondering if you could download Viber app on your phone

[Boom! And away we cull!]

Its very fast and better

-I'm sorry. I can't. I broke my good phone so I'm using my work phone and I'm not allowed to download anything

OK can I have your phone number so I could call you?

[Second try to get me alone.]

-I don't mind chatting on this

-No. Work phone. It's not really mine and they monitor it

OK that's ok

[Notice how many times they all say this?]

You at work now?

-Hey. I'm way behind. Can we chat later. Yes I am at work

Take a picture of you and send it to me

[His attempt to see if I'm a legit target and not out to frame him.]

I want to see you at work now

-I'll get fired. If I had my phone I would

Na wa o

[I googled this – it means "damn" "wtf" "unbelievable" "pitiful" in Nigerian.]

C fmt

[No idea – perhaps one of you could tell me?]

-What?

What's your birth sign?

-Cancer. Tell me yours then I really got to go

OK no problem

[Didn't tell me his sign...]

We talk later

[No further communication from him.]

* * *

When I first opened my social media author account, I had over a dozen of these scammers contact me. I even got a message from a person posing as a previous Colonels I met when I was married to an Army officer – the picture just happened to be one of a GEN... or COL who was our Commander in Ft. Carson... or maybe NY... or Ft. Benning. I can't recall, but I recognized him. His wife gave us a picture book about pigs when one of my daughters was born. It was their signature baby gift.

Also, three other officers I personally know have had their image stolen for these romance scams. I trolled all of these scammers for a while before I blocked them.

To reiterate the usual tells: They call you love, dear, or sweetie right off. They ask weird questions like, "what's your favorite color?" and "what do you fear?"

They say they're in the military, but don't know any military terminology, or think an SSG is an officer. They have no idea what an NCO is, and most of the time they're not specific about what military branch they're in, or what their MOS is.

One scammer said he was from New Orleans. I asked how the weather was in Louisiana, and he had no idea what I was asking – he was genuinely confused.

They all (usually) portray themselves as widowed and have one or two children - boy or girl - age range from six to sixteen. Most wives die in a car accident. One died in a car accident but she didn't have her inhaler on her, so she actually died from asthma. One "was late" in a plane crash. One "was late" in a car crash. A "fire" accident is a fairly new way to die. They seemingly know our terminology, but apparently not how to use it in casual conversation.

If not military, they pose as engineers or doctors and are currently in another country working – away from their child(ren). One dude told me he was from Austria. I mentioned Arnold, and he had no idea who I was talking about – said he never left New Orleans.

They don't know our movie or political icons, and their sentence structure is off. Educated engineers and doctors who can't put together a sentence? I don't believe it, and you shouldn't either.

Another dude said he was stuck in his office

Sandra Miller Linhart

and needed me to send him a $50 prepaid card. They start off small, apparently, and then move in for the kill.

They're out there. Don't be fooled. And they're not only on one social media. I received this next beauty on a completely different one:

Ryan Ragsdale

Hi beautiful how are you doing, And how has your day been, I'm sure you must be wondering who I am, Well I'm Ryan Ragsdale by name live in Alabama and I'm just a man who want to make friends cause am kind of new don't know much about it. I must say you really look beautiful on your pic I will have to go now hope to hear from you soon

-Hello. I'm doing well. Thank you for the kind words.

You welcome

I'm Ryan by name and you..?

[Well, Ryan by name...]

-I can't find your profile on FB. Can you send me a link?

I block it my self for security reason am only here to chat with family and friends if you want a picture of my I can send you okay hope you don't mind

[Notice the okay.]

-What do you do for a living? Tell me a little about yourself, as I block for security reasons, too and would like to know who I am chatting with before I chat.

Okay I'm Ryan by name live in Mobil Alabama, I'm a widower I lost my wife 6 years ago in a car accident and have a 14 years old daughter name Olivia. I'm a drilling engineering in a oil drilling ship in Scotland US as a oil drilling Supervisor

[I didn't realize Scotland was part of the US, and it's 'Mobile' the last I checked.]

Okay your turn tell me a little about you?

* * *

I'd heard enough and blocked his message. His was one of the first encounters I'd had with these vermin, or I may have played along a bit more.

As I said earlier: Term of endearment/flattery. Check! Widow. Check! Wife died [in car accident]. Check! One kid between the ages of six and sixteen. Check! Engineer. Check! Out of country. Check! Not too keen with American English and random punctuation. Check!

Other things that waved a red flag: he contacted me on my author social media page. It has my name all over the place. In the message, he asks me my name. He says he doesn't know much about it (the social media platform? life? making friends?), but then says he blocks his social media page for security reasons and only uses it to chat with family and friends.

This information only adds up to scam city, and it practically writes itself.

Getting Help

Unfortunately, there's no real help out there for someone who's been scammed. Hopefully you've read this book, or one like it before the scammer took anything tangible or intangible from you.

The first time I was approached by one of these guys I was new to that specific social media platform. I thought it was a bit strange someone would private message me there with the leading line, "Hello, Dear." I am ashamed to admit I almost fell for his ploy. Enough so that I downloaded Viber (I've since deleted the app.) and sent him a snap of me (pg rated, for sure). Then, luckily, I was soon approached by another "man" who was also a widower with a child and red flags started popping up all over the place. I did some research into their claims and immediately reported them.

The social medias give us options to report these jerks – they each have a button under the settings to block and report a profile. Ensure you report him first, then block because once you block you can't always report. The last time I reported a scammer, the platform blocked him automatically.

I highly suggest you report these guys as soon as you suspect them as scammers so the social media platform in which they prey can investigate and shut them down before they defraud another lonely soul.

You can rest assured you're not the only lamb they have in their barn. If the social media platform shuts them down, they have to start all over with a new profile – and hopefully they've not had time to cull too many of their victims from the herd.

Protect yourself. Don't friend anyone you don't personally know. If they show up as a friend of a friend, ask your friend about this person before accepting the stranger's request. Many of our friends blindly accept friend requests from anyone without discretion. The scammer now has a new set of names he can scam by posing as your friend's friend.

Some websites and social media pages have been set up to help identify and warn of potential scammers. There are a myriad popping up daily so I can't realistically list any here. Search on 'Internet scammers' and quite a few links should show up for you.

If you have been scammed out of a significant amount of money, or if someone is terrorizing you, contact the FBI and report the crime. They can offer you advice on what to do next. Your local law enforcement has no power outside their jurisdiction. The best they can do is warn others.

Most importantly, get informed and realize you're not alone. Some of these guys are exceptional at trickery. Many of the ones who contacted me were obvious amateurs, and fairly easy to spot. There are more experienced jerks out there. So be cautious.

One of the better ones had contacted me and I strung him along for a while to ensure he was a scammer – he was simply that good at it. There were times during our conversation I thought he could be legit, but then he gave a tell and I blocked him. He was good; he nearly had me at 'Hello, Love'

Please keep in mind that even though you may be lonely, you're not alone in this. Be safe, be diligent, and stay whole.

* * *

While writing this booklet I attempted to keep useful information to a minimum, just in case a scammer reads it. The last thing I want to do is present a real how-to guide to these bastards.

Explaining what sentence structure or words the average American would use, or describing in detail military protocol would give these faux Casanovas an invaluable tool to make their deceit more believable. The goal of this book, of course, is the opposite.

If have any suggestions, comments, or questions, you may email me at <u>sandra@sandstarbooks.com</u>. I truly hope you found this booklet amusing if not helpful.

About the Author

Sandra Miller Linhart was born and raised in a somewhat isolated, but beautiful, mountainous town in Wyoming. There she cultivated her love of the written word, as the nearest decent record store was a good two-hour drive away and the one local radio station played only country and classical music at that time. Were it not for that, Ms. Linhart might today be a rock star, or, at the very least have better taste in music.

As it turned out, Lander provided a well-stocked and constantly updated library. Thus, the young Ms. Linhart often found herself taking long journeys into the wonderful worlds created by authors like Ursula K. LeGuin, Judy Blume, Madeleine L'Engle, Stephen King and, of course, Erma Bombeck in the dusty basement which contained the children's section of the Fremont County Public Library.

Sandra then traveled the country as a military wife and mother of five army brats; soaking in our country's diverse and obscure cultural differences—which makes wonderful fodder for her stories.

She currently lives in the mountains of Colorado but spends a majority of her time at the beach.

Sandra writes in hopes of sharing her love of reading and writing with everyone. She utilizes her sociology degree and personal experience in writing children's books for caregivers, parents, and children to better connect and communicate, with the goal of healing anxieties and fears. She loves to write for children of all ages, and plans to do so until her last page is turned.

Life (and how *you* live it) is her inspiration. Visit her website: www.sandstarbooks.com

www.ingramcontent.com/pod-product-compliance
Lightning Source LLC
Chambersburg PA
CBHW060517280326
41933CB00014B/3005